J. Edgar Hoover, FBI director, 1924-1972

The FBI building in Washington, D.C. is on the corner of Pennsylvania Avenue and 10th Street.

Cornerstones of Freedom

The Story of
THE FBI

By Jim Hargrove

CHILDRENS PRESS ®

CHICAGO

The FBI building is named after J. Edgar Hoover, who ran the bureau for forty-eight years.

Library of Congress Cataloging-in-Publication Data

Hargrove, Jim.
  The story of the FBI.

  (Cornerstones of freedom)
  Summary: A brief history of the investigative
division of the United States Justice Department.
  1. United States. Federal Bureau of Investigation—
Juvenile literature. [1. United States. Federal
Bureau of Investigation] I. Title. II. Series.
HV1841.H296 1988   353.0074   87-36815
ISBN 0-516-04733-7

Childrens Press®, Chicago
Copyright ©1988 by Regensteiner Publishing Enterprises, Inc.
All rights reserved. Published simultaneously in Canada.
Printed in the United States of America.
  3 4 5 6 7 8 9 10 R 97 96 95 94 93 92 91 90 89

In the early part of 1982, Special Agent Bill O'Keefe of the Federal Bureau of Investigation began working on a very unusual case. He was visiting organizations in the Washington, D.C. area that worked on secret projects for the United States government. Some were defense contractors, people who build weapons and other types of machinery for the armed forces. Others performed various services related to the government's efforts to defend American interests from foreign attack.

Agent O'Keefe made an unusual request during his visits. Each time, he asked a high-level boss if there might be an employee willing to sell American secrets to Russian spies. Not surprisingly, he had difficulty finding anyone, boss or employee, who would agree to such a thing.

After he was turned down at eighteen different companies and organizations, Agent O'Keefe went to the Riverside Research Institute. At the institute people study the problems of tracking missiles in flight high above the earth. O'Keefe knew that a number of employees there had secret information that would be of great interest to Russian spies.

After a lengthy talk O'Keefe discovered that Riverside's chief of security, a forty-five-year-old man named John Stine, was willing to help. Following the FBI agent's advice, Stine would try to sell

The Pentagon, headquarters of the U.S. Department of Defense, covers twenty-nine acres in Arlington, Virginia.

papers to spies working for the communist government of Russia.

For nearly a year, Stine, O'Keefe, and other FBI agents worked out a dangerous plan in a locked and darkened hotel room near Washington. Gradually, they developed a phony story that they hoped would fool a Russian agent. They decided to make it appear as if Stine, Riverside's chief of security, had a number of serious problems, including alcoholism and a habit of gambling away large amounts of money. They hoped that the false impression might convince Russian spies that Stine was desperate enough to sell American secrets to them.

Agent O'Keefe worked with U.S. officials in the Pentagon to decide what kinds of secrets Stine should try to sell to the Russians. After some time Pentagon officials selected some papers in the Riverside office that could be handed over to the Russians without endangering U.S. security.

When all the plans of the operation were finally completed, it was nearly Thanksgiving Day of 1982. On the evening before Thanksgiving, a number of FBI agents took Stine out to a Washington bar and got him drunk. When he woke up the next day, O'Keefe reasoned, Stine would have a hangover and be able to play his role as a boozing gambler more convincingly.

The next morning, as Stine put gray dye in his hair and pasted on a fake moustache, he could feel his head ache. A number of papers and documents from the Riverside Research Institute, each marked SECRET, were taped to his body underneath his sweater. Agent O'Keefe watched out of a hotel room window as Stine got into a taxicab and headed toward the Soviet Military Office, one of a number of Russian government offices in Washington.

Stine remained inside the Soviet office building for more than six hours. Only later did O'Keefe learn that the phony story seemed to have worked. Although the Russians first protested that they were

Soviet Embassy and military offices in Washington, D.C.

only diplomats uninterested in the work of spies, they eventually gave Stine five hundred dollars for the papers he brought them. More importantly, they offered Stine the chance to do more spying against the U.S. government. Stine was told to be in a phone booth in a Washington suburb in Virginia in exactly six weeks to await more instructions.

During the next six weeks, Stine and O'Keefe were careful not to be seen in public. When the specified time arrived on January 19, 1983, Stine was at the phone booth, but no call came. Instead, a Russian agent contacted him at home, telling him to do the same thing the next day. This time the phone rang. Stine was told to drive immediately to another phone booth, about twenty miles away in Maryland. The call came just as Stine approached the new booth. He was instructed to find a crushed pack of cigarettes a few steps away. Inside the package was a written list of new instructions to be followed immediately. The instructions eventually led him to a wire fence near a shopping center. There he was given a pop can stuffed with money and new instructions by a Russian agent posing as a jogger.

The instructions told Stine to make photographs of secret documents. The rolls of film were to be placed inside a garbage bag and dropped in a rural area of Maryland on Saturday, April 9. O'Keefe and other FBI agents were disappointed that the delivery time was so far away. They had hoped to make the operation move more quickly. They decided to wrap up the case on April 9, but they were disappointed. Although a Russian agent repeatedly drove by the Maryland site at the appointed time, he eventually returned to Washington without stopping.

Stine received a phone call from a Russian agent the next morning, instructing him to do the same thing the following Saturday. Stine once again did as he was told. He placed rolls of film in a garbage bag, drove to the deserted road in Maryland, and dropped the bag in the tall weeds by the roadside. Just as had been true a week earlier, Stine was not

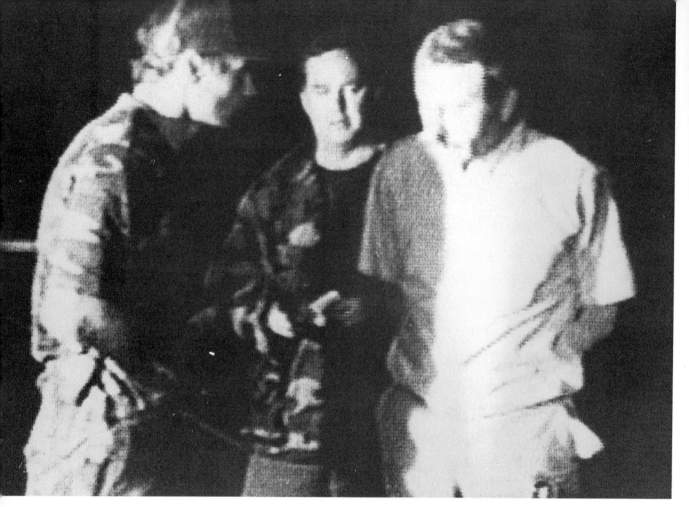

Videotape shows FBI agents arresting a Russian agent.

alone. Nine FBI agents hid in ditches and behind trees waiting for the Russian spy to claim the film.

In time, a blue car pulled up to the site and stopped. A middle-aged man in a red jacket and blue jeans stepped out of the car and found the garbage bag in the weeds. But as soon as he picked up the bag, O'Keefe and the other FBI agents leaped up from their hiding places, blinding the spy with their bright flashlights. The Russian was immediately told that he was under arrest for espionage.

Colonel Izmaylov was expelled from the United States in 1986.

After more than a year of careful planning, special agent O'Keefe had caught Yevgeny Barmyantsev, an important Russian military official, in the act of trying to buy American secrets. Because Barmyantsev enjoyed what is called diplomatic immunity, he could not be placed on trial, but he was deported. Another Soviet agent, identified by the FBI men during the same operation, was called back to Russia soon afterward.

John Stine continued working at the Riverside Research Institute. For a while he received a number of crank phone calls, which he assumed were from angry Russian agents. But the calls eventually stopped. Bill O'Keefe continued looking for other Russian agents working in the Washington area. In 1986 he captured another Russian spy, Colonel Vladimir Izmaylov, in a similar operation. Although it all may sound a bit like a spy novel, this is part of the real work of the FBI, the investigative division of the U.S. Justice Department.

The organization that eventually became the FBI was formed in 1908. At the time President Theodore Roosevelt was trying to combat people who were illegally selling public land in the American West, as well as a number of big business abuses in the East. The Department of Justice, the chief law enforcement branch of the United States government, had the authority to stop the illegal acts. But it lacked the people needed to investigate the crimes and to identify suspects. Although the Justice Department occasionally borrowed Secret Service agents from the U.S. Treasury Department, the practice was banned by Congress in 1908.

A year earlier, in 1907, the attorney general, the head of the Justice Department, noted that "a Department of Justice with no force of permanent police in any form under its control is assuredly not fully equipped for its work." By 1908 it was clear that the Justice Department did not have the type of people it needed to enforce the sometimes complicated laws related to the land and business abuses President Theodore Roosevelt was trying to stop.

After a number of angry encounters with Congress, President Roosevelt took matters into his own hands. He ordered his attorney general to create an investigative service within the Department of

Charles J. Bonaparte

William Howard Taft

Justice. Attorney General Charles J. Bonaparte
issued an order on July 26, 1908, which allowed the
Justice Department to hire a small group of detec-
tives. Less than a year later, during the administration of President William Howard Taft, the group
was officially named the Bureau of Investigation.

Technicians at work in the FBI crime laboratory

During its earliest years, the responsibilities of the bureau grew rapidly. It was charged with enforcing federal laws, which often meant investigating interstate crimes; in other words, catching suspected criminals who moved across state lines to avoid prosecution. The bureau was involved in a number of celebrated manhunts in its early years and broke up several international and interstate white slave (forced prostitution) rings.

But the bureau had problems that limited its effectiveness. Agents were not held to strict standards of behavior. The Justice Department, headquartered in Washington, had little control over its agents scattered around the country. Many agents were controlled by local politicians, who often used them to advance their own interests.

Four people were killed and hundreds injured in the Black Tom explosion.

By the year 1915, when World War I was raging in Europe, the Bureau of Investigation had a total of 219 agents. Undertrained and poorly supervised, they were ordered to catch an army of German spies sent to America to blow up U.S. ammunition dumps and burn food supplies. Despite the bureau's efforts, a German spy blew up America's largest arsenal on the Black Tom River near New York City, on July 30, 1916. The blasts damaged many of the buildings in Manhattan and were heard one hundred miles away.

When America entered World War I in 1917, the bureau was quickly increased to four hundred men. During the war years, Bureau of Investigation agents arrested more than six thousand enemy aliens, but only about a third were actually jailed.

When news of the Russian communist revolution became widespread, the bureau also added investigations of suspected American communists to its many duties. During the years following World War I, the bureau did much to break the power of the anti-Negro, anti-Jewish, anti-Catholic terrorist organization known as the Ku Klux Klan.

Ku Klux Klansmen gather before a burning cross, a KKK symbol.

William J. Burns

Warren G. Harding

World War I had been over for three years when, in 1921, Warren G. Harding became president of the United States. Harding's attorney general, Harry Daugherty, appointed a new director for the bureau, a famous detective named William J. Burns. Appointed assistant director was twenty-six-year-old J. Edgar Hoover, who had previously worked as special assistant to the attorney general.

The administration of Warren G. Harding was rocked by one of the worst political scandals in American history. Government oil fields in Wyoming, collectively called Teapot Dome, were illegally leased to a private businessman. Albert Fall, the secretary of the interior, had accepted a large bribe as part of the illegal transaction. President Harding died of an illness on August 2, 1923, but the investigation into the Teapot Dome scandal continued under the administration of President Calvin Coolidge.

Charges were also made that Attorney General Harry Daugherty, the Bureau of Investigation's overseer, was also involved in the scandal. The U.S. Senate conducted hearings to look into the matter. During the investigation, a friend of bureau director Burns testified that the director had ordered his agents to spy on the senators themselves. The agents, he testified, broke into senators' offices, read their mail and personal papers, followed them around Washington, and tried to find anything incriminating that could be used to stop the Senate's investigation into the dealings of Attorney General Daugherty.

Investigations and court cases involving the Teapot Dome scandal dragged on for years. But Americans by the millions were disgusted with their

J. Edgar Hoover in 1926
at the age of 31

government, in general, and the Bureau of Investigation, in particular. On May 9, 1924, William J. Burns resigned as director of the Bureau of Investigation. President Coolidge and Attorney General Harlan Fiske Stone had already agreed on his replacement. On May 10, 1924, twenty-nine-year-old J. Edgar Hoover was told that he was about to become the new acting director of the Bureau of Investigation.

At the time many people throughout the nation were calling for the bureau to disband. But Hoover was convinced that the tide of public opinion could be turned if he cleaned up the organization, and that is exactly what he began to do. Suddenly, agents across the country were surprised to find a long series of tough, clear instructions from the new director placed in their mailboxes. Agents were told that immoral behavior of any sort would not be tolerated. They were reminded that their sole duty was to investigate violations of federal laws, not to perform political favors or enjoy personal gain.

Hoover also worked with the U.S. Congress, asking senators and representatives not to use appointments to the bureau as political rewards. At the same time, he reviewed the personnel file of every agent in the bureau, firing anyone who appeared incompetent or unfair. For those who remained, he devised a strict code of conduct. Among many other rules, the new code let agents know that they would be fired immediately if they used brutality when conducting an investigation, drank liquor while working, or used a government car for anything other than official business.

During the same year, an act of Congress created the bureau's identification division. At the time, more than 800,000 fingerprints were forwarded to the bureau's Washington headquarters from the Bureau of Criminal Identification in Chicago and from the U.S. Penitentiary in Leavenworth, Kansas. The fingerprint files grew rapidly over the years. Today, fingerprints from nearly half the people in the United States are on file in the FBI's huge identification division.

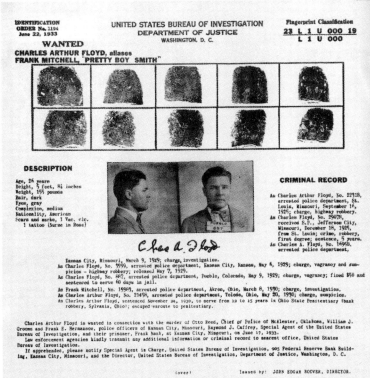

By 1943 there were about 68 million sets of fingerprints on file. About 100,000 were arriving daily. Photographs and fingerprints of criminals wanted by the FBI (left) were posted in public places throughout the United States.

On December 10, 1924, the word *acting* was removed from Hoover's title. He now became director of the Bureau of Investigation. J. Edgar Hoover remained the bureau's director for forty-eight years, until his death in 1972 at the age of seventy-seven. During that time he transformed the agency from an unsophisticated and scandal-ridden organization to one of the world's largest and most resourceful investigative bureaus.

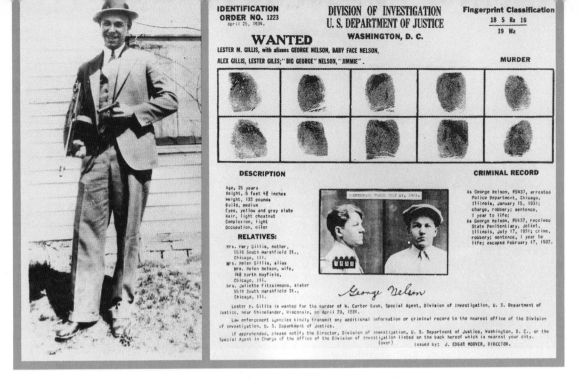

John Dillinger (left) and "Baby Face" Nelson (right)

During the early years of his tenure, Hoover began recruiting agents with advanced college degrees, usually in law or accounting. He established uniform policies across the nation so that agents, regardless of their location, would know exactly what was expected of them. He also established a school so that new recruits could be trained extensively in FBI methods.

As the years passed, bureau agents were given new responsibilities. Congress gave agents the authority to carry guns and make arrests. During the 1930s the bureau broke up many of the criminal gangs left over from the Prohibition Era of the 1920s. The work of FBI agents was critical in ending the careers of such notorious gangsters as John

Dillinger, "Baby Face" Nelson, and "Pretty Boy" Floyd. The scope of federal crimes, which gave the bureau authority to investigate, was expanded to include bank robbery, kidnapping, extortion, and other criminal activities. In 1935 Congress officially changed the bureau's name to its present form, the Federal Bureau of Investigation.

With J. Edgar Hoover's continuing leadership, the FBI became one of the most popular and respected branches of the government during the 1930s and 1940s. FBI agents were popularly called G-men (the *G* stood for *government*) and were widely regarded as heroes. Children played games in the afternoon in which FBI agents chased criminals and then went to bed at night proudly wearing "junior G-man" pajamas.

As the FBI's role gained wide public acceptance, Hoover established the huge FBI laboratory, which

Agents are trained to recognize specific features of the criminals they pursue.

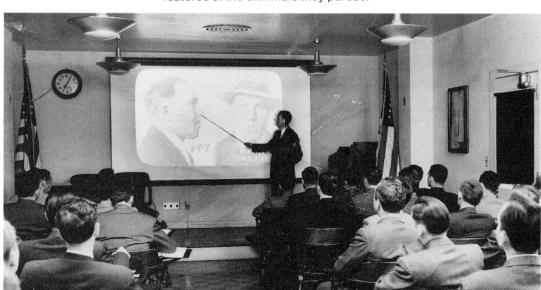

Agents learn to shoot at the National Academy
(left). In 1942 FBI agents broke
the Duquesne spy ring (above).

brought the latest advances in scientific research
into the fight against crime. In 1935, a time when
many people were demanding the creation of a
national police force, Hoover created the FBI
National Academy, which trained local police
officers in the up-to-date techniques of the bureau.

Just how far the FBI had advanced since World
War I was demonstrated clearly during the years of
the Second World War. From 1939 to 1945 not a
single case of sabotage by Nazi or Japanese agents
occurred anywhere in the continental United States.
Most of the spy rings operating in the country were
smashed by the FBI prior to America's entry into
World War II. In highly secret operations, President Franklin Roosevelt authorized the FBI to enter
a number of Central and South American nations.
There, agents broke up extensive Nazi spy rings and
captured shortwave radios that were pumping vital
war information directly to Nazi Germany.

After World War II, FBI agents investigated alleged communists in the United States. As early as 1936, President Roosevelt had given the bureau secret orders to investigate communist activity in America. J. Edgar Hoover, for many years a devout anticommunist, was eager to use the FBI's considerable resources to investigate the communist party and its sympathizers.

In the late 1940s and the 1950s, many real soviet spies, including some involved in stealing secrets about the atomic bomb, were apprehended. But some people have charged that, in its efforts to expose communists, the bureau sometimes went too far, investigating many individuals whose only crime seemed to be a difference of opinion from that of Director Hoover or a distrust of the FBI itself. Nevertheless, the bureau's work ending the careers of genuine communist spies has been invaluable.

Beginning in 1957 under the administration of President Eisenhower, the U.S. Congress passed the first of many laws designed to protect the civil rights of Americans, especially members of minority groups. From that time on, FBI agents began a vigorous civil rights campaign, as Director Hoover put it, "to ensure that no citizen is deprived of the free exercise or enjoyment of any right or privilege secured to him by the Constitution. . . ."

In January of 1967 the enormous National Crime Information Center (CIC) was established at FBI headquarters in Washington. One of the world's largest computerized data centers, the CIC maintains millions of files on criminals and criminal activities. Because electronically stored data can be recovered so quickly, FBI records could be used to assist local police departments within minutes of a request for information. A year after the CIC was formed, work began on new facilities for the FBI National Academy, established in 1935. Work on the ultra-modern facility was completed in 1972.

Computer at the National Crime Information Center in 1967

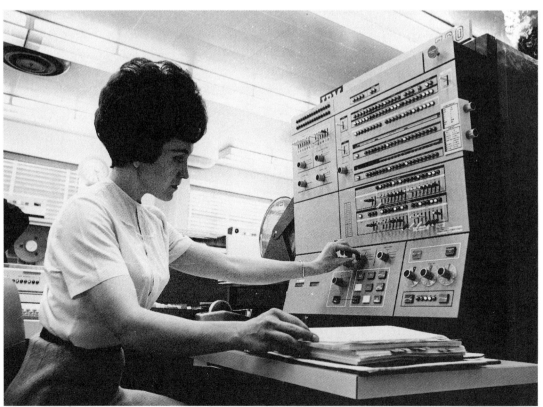

The American protest movement of the late 1960s seemed to grow out of the civil rights movement and, of course, opposition to the Vietnam War. The FBI vigorously investigated all protest groups, sometimes, critics claimed, with little regard to their actual threat to the security of the United States. Although it had rendered invaluable service to the nation, the FBI was once again the source of some controversy.

But despite his critics, FBI Director J. Edgar Hoover had ample reason to be proud of his accomplishments. In a typical year during the late 1960s, FBI agents caught nearly 19,000 fugitives resulting in more than 13,000 criminal convictions; recovered more than 22,000 stolen motor vehicles; and made available hundreds of thousands of details about criminal activities to various local police agencies.

In addition to its Washington headquarters, the bureau had field offices in 59 cities as well as 526 smaller offices serving all 50 states and Puerto Rico. Offices were maintained in 11 cities around the world. In all, the FBI employed more than 7,000 special agents and more than 9,000 others. Although its annual budget amounted to almost $200 million, the FBI actually earned more than that amount in recovered merchandise, money, and criminal fines resulting from its investigations.

After nearly a half century of service as FBI director, J. Edgar Hoover died in May of 1972. Mr. Hoover was replaced by L. Patrick Gray, who held the office for only a year. Although Gray introduced a number of reforms, including allowing women to become FBI special agents for the first time, he came to office at a time of great political upheaval.

Just one month after Gray became FBI director, it was discovered that men working for the reelection of President Nixon had broken into the national headquarters of the Democratic Party in the Watergate Hotel in Washington. In 1973 Gray admitted that he had destroyed important papers found in the safe of a Watergate burglar. He resigned and was replaced by Clarence Kelley.

Clarence Kelley

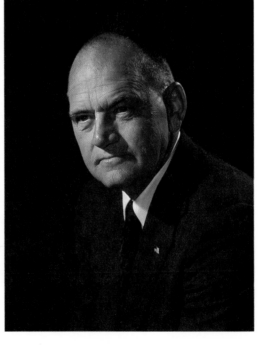

L. Patrick Gray

National Academy firing range (left),
and the weapons lab (above)

In 1975 a lengthy Senate investigation revealed
some serious wrongdoings that had been committed
by the bureau under the directorship of J. Edgar
Hoover. It was charged, for example, that FBI
agents had helped a number of presidents, including
Roosevelt, Kennedy, Johnson, and Nixon investigate
the private lives of their political opponents. Agents
had been involved in illegal wiretaps, hundreds of
unconstitutional burglaries, and even kidnappings.
Because he disliked civil rights leader Dr. Martin
Luther King, Jr., Hoover had ordered his phone
tapped dozens of times and had had a letter sent to
him suggesting that he commit suicide. It was even
charged that FBI agents had destroyed evidence
relating to the assassination of President Kennedy.

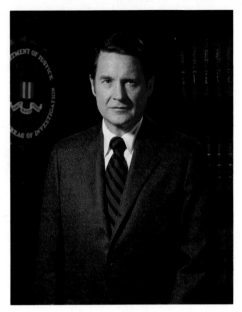

William H. Webster

William S. Sessions

In 1976 Director Kelley made a public apology for the bureau's past mistakes. Working with the Justice Department, he began drafting new rules to try to prevent such abuses from happening again.

In 1978, under the administration of President Jimmy Carter, William H. Webster became the new director of the FBI. The following year members of the U.S. Congress and the Justice Department wrote a lengthy new charter for the bureau, describing exactly how it was expected to perform in the future. Webster remained director of the Bureau until 1987, when he became director of the Central Intelligence Agency. On August 3, 1987, William S. Sessions, a former judge, became the new director of the FBI.

The work of the FBI is often as saddening as it is exciting and dangerous. Agents of the FBI must often see people at their worst and must try to bring them to justice. At the same time, agents—and Americans in general—must work to see that the vast powers of the Federal Bureau of Investigation are used wisely, even under difficult circumstances. It is an unending struggle.

FBI training session

PHOTO CREDITS

About the Author

Jim Hargrove has worked as a writer and editor for more than ten years. After serving as an editorial director for three Chicago area publishers, he began a career as an independent writer, preparing a series of books for children. He has contributed to works by nearly twenty different publishers. His Childrens Press titles include biographies of Mark Twain and Richard Nixon. With his wife and daughter, he lives in a small Illinois town near the Wisconsin border.